SUPER POWERS

Jeremy Dobrish

BROADWAY PLAY PUBLISHING INC
224 E 62nd St, NY, NY 10065
www.broadwayplaypub.com
info@broadwayplaypub.com

SUPERPOWERS

First printing: July 2005
I S B N: 0-88145-264-5

Book design: Marie Donovan
Word processing: Microsoft Word
Typographic controls: Xerox Ventura Publisher 2.0 P E
Typeface: Palatino
Printed and bound in the U S A

SUPERPOWERS ws first presented by adobe theatre company (Jeremy Dobrish, Artistic Director; Christopher Roberts, Producing Director) at The Ohio Theater (N Y C) on 21 April 2004. The cast and creative contributors were:

SAM/DON/SAMPSON	Arthur Aulisi
JUNIOR/EVAN/WOOFER	Jeremy Brisiel
JONATHAN	Ryan Bronz
DANA	Nina Hellman
ABE	Stan Lachow
CATHY	Christy Meyer
ESTHER/CYNTHIA/MARLENE	Dana Smith-Croll
KALEF	Margie Stokley

Director	Jessica Davis-Irons
Scenic design	Neal Wilkinson
Lighting design	Michael Gottlieb
Original music & sound design	Jill B C DuBoff
Costume design	Meganne George
Video design	Sze Lin Pang
Properties	Sarah Krainin
Stage manager	Alexis R Prussack
General management	Performance Associates
Production Coordinator	Janine L Pangburn
Press representative	Jeffrey Richards Associates

CHARACTERS

JONATHAN, *thirties*
CATHY, *thirties*
ABE, *sixties*
KALEF, *thirties*
DANA, *thirties*
SAM/DON/SAMPSON/GUARD, *forties*
JUNIOR/EVAN/WOOFER, *thirties*
ESTHER/CYNTHIA/MARLENE, *fifties*

A note for the actors: a "/" in the middle of a sentence indicates that the next actor should start speaking. The words following the "/" should trail off and the next actors line should overtake.

A note for the actors playing KALEF *and* WOOFER *(who are dogs): don't imitate a dog. Be dog-like. Have dogish qualities but be a human dog.*

The actors playing ABE *and* CATHY *must also basically play two different versions of each of these characters.*

Regarding the set and production, each section needs to flow along with one location melding and blurring into the next. Sorry. By all means don't fully realize anywhere. That would be tragic.

A reminder to the reader: no matter what JONATHAN, CATHY *and* ABE *say about themselves or how they act, they still appear outwardly as a visible young man, a plain looking woman and an older man respectively. In addition,* KALEF, *no matter what choice is made with costumes and make-up will always appear in some way human.*

PROLOGUE:
A POLICE ROOM

(A long table. Chairs. MARLENE *[a female cop] sits at the table rubbing her head. Sitting on the table, with their legs crossed, staring out at the audience are:* ABE *[a man in his sixties],* JONTHAN *[a naked man in his thirties. N B—* JONTHAN *could be "naked" and still wear some sort of flesh colored underpants or something if desired. He needs to read as naked more than he actually needs to be naked], and* CATHY *[a plain looking woman in her thirties).*

*(*MARLENE *rubs her head.* DON *[a male cop] appears in the door. Neither* DON *nor* MARLENE *notice the other three.)*

DON: Hey.

*(*MARLENE *looks up.)*

MARLENE: Yeah?

DON: Y'O K?

MARLENE: What? Yeah. Tired. *(What's up?)* What?

*(*DON *throws a file onto the table.)*

DON: Accident.

MARLENE: Type?

DON: Car. Read.

MARLENE: What's it say?

DON: Old guy. Drives Porsche. Too fast. Hits woman.

MARLENE: Dead?

DON: Hospital.

MARLENE: So?

(She tosses the file back to him.)

DON: There's more.

MARLENE: Yeah?

DON: Hits dog. Kills it.

MARLENE: K.

DON: There's more. Hits a...guy too.

MARLENE: Yeah?

DON: He's naked.

MARLENE: A naked man walking down the streets of New York?

DON: Yup.

MARLENE: Interesting.

DON: Yup.

MARLENE: Why?

DON: Naked?

MARLENE: Yeah.

DON: Don't know. Comes through, we'll ask.

MARLENE: Weird. Eyewitnesses?

DON: One. Being questioned. Word is—unreliable.

MARLENE: How so.

DON: Don't know. Just his...words don't...add up.

MARLENE: Happened fast.

DON: Asshole.

MARLENE: Eyewitness?

DON: Driver.

MARLENE: Why?

DON: Drives like that? Asshole.

MARLENE: Keep me...

DON: posted?

MARLENE: Yeah.

DON: Will do. *(He exits.)*

*(*ABE, JONTHAN *and* CATHY *look at each other, a tad confused.)*

*(*CATHY *and* JONTHAN *turn to* ABE.*)*

(A spotlight hits ABE. *He speaks with a slight Eastern European accent. As he does the others exit as the stage s set for:)*

SECTION 1: ABE'S APARTMENT, A DINER, A PSYCHIATRIST'S OFFICE, A CAR SHOWROOM, INSIDE A CAR

ABE: Asshole is an unfair word for someone you've not met. A judgement on a story you've not heard. But fine. I'll start. I'll tell my story. Though. "Start". How does one start? Whatever I might say would lead me back a step, and then again another step. Should I start with I was born sixty something years ago in Brooklyn to immigrants? This would only take me to my parents and their story and so on and so on. The only thing this proves is that I have good genes. That all my ancestors did live until an age when they could procreate, and then they procreated with success. Since the start of time. But fine. There was a crash. My car. I am guilty, yes, I guess. I drove the car and so I must be guilty. I am guilty of so many things but that does not suggest that any of this is my fault. And that is a distinction. Guilt

and fault. Guilt I know. Fault... The fault is in our stars.
But fine. We need a start, so let's look for a start.
I choose the start to be not birth, but death. And yet.
I can't start there. For that would kill me. Again.
So I'll start here.

*(*ABE *moves to his apartment and sits.* SAM *[*ABE*'s son] enters and sits near* ABE*. They sit in silence for a moment.)*

SAM: Is it...do you want me to go?

ABE: Go. Stay.

(Pause)

SAM: How's...what's his name...your neighbor...

ABE: Who?

SAM: Bill. How is Bill?

ABE: Who cares? I don't. You don't.

SAM: Dad. *(Pause)* Dad, you have got to continue on with your life. How long has it been?

ABE: Eight months next Tuesday.

SAM: But who's counting?

ABE: I shouldn't count? My wife of forty six years dies and I shouldn't count each day, each wretched day?

SAM: I'm worried about you. This is a quintessential, classic / case of...

ABE: I'll be fine. A son doesn't worry about his father. There's three things you should never need in life: a good doctor, a good lawyer

ABE & SAM: ...and a good son

SAM: I know, I know,

ABE: You don't worry about me. I worry about you. You may be Mister Published Therapist Leader-In-His-

Field Mister, talky-talky man but you're still a little Pisha.

SAM: You have to let the grief out and begin to get your/ life back.

ABE: I'm a lucky man. I had a lucky life. I had a long time with your Mother. You take what you're dealt.

SAM: And that's it?

ABE: Stop it.

(Pause)

SAM: My therapist says...

ABE: You have a therapist?

SAM: Of course.

ABE: You ARE a therapist.

SAM: All the more reason that I require / one.

ABE: Fine, fine, I don't care. I don't care what he says....

SAM: She

ABE: ...I don't care what you say.

SAM: Do you regret marrying her?

ABE: What!?

SAM: If you knew she would pass away first would you have married someone else?

ABE: Don't talk like that.

SAM: Why not? Everyone wants someone to take care of them when they / get older.

ABE: First of all, it's not realistic. You can't have such choices so why play such games?

SAM: It's a hypothetical, which can be very useful in / opening up...

ABE: Second of all how dare you ask me that? I love your Mother more than anything in the world. More than you if you want to know the truth. She loved you more, like a Mother should, but she was my whole life. So don't you dare ask me if I would forsake her.

SAM: Right. *(Pause)* Is...?

ABE: Stop.

SAM: Is...?

ABE: Stop.

SAM: What?

ABE: Talking. Must you talk?

(Pause)

SAM: Yes. Is there nothing you regret? Nothing you'd do differently?

ABE: Regret is useless.

SAM: That doesn't make it unreal.

ABE: Stop it.

SAM: What?

ABE: Talking. Like that.

SAM: Like what?

ABE: Like you always talk.

SAM: So you're telling me you wouldn't wish for anything to be different in your life?

ABE: My only...

SAM: Yes?

ABE: My only wish would be that when I was young I should have the wisdom of age, and when I'm old, I should have the body of youth.

SAM: Why? What would you have done with wisdom?

ABE: Will you stop with me?

SAM: What would you do with a younger body?

ABE: What would I do? Why is the sky blue? Why are people mean to each other? What is love? Where do we go when we die? Will you never stop asking me ridiculous questions?

SAM: Tell me. What would you do?

ABE: I would...

SAM: ...

ABE: I don't know. Enjoy myself. Take a trip.

SAM: So take a trip.

ABE: What's the point?

SAM: To enjoy. Not taking the trip, that's regret. We don't regret the things we do, we regret the things we don't do.

ABE: You read that in a book?

SAM: No, I wrote it in one.

ABE: Figures.

SAM: You have money saved up. You never spent on anything. God forbid the M T A went up a quarter it was the apocalypse. You never indulged yourself. I mean I wish you could see yourself. Is this how you wanted to end up? You always told Mom "One day we'll do this. One day we'll go here." Do you know she talked about that Alaska cruise every time I called? She thought it would be beautiful. But there was always a reason to postpone, And so now she's out of days. So what are you going to do: just die with whatever money you've saved up? I don't need it. Spend it. Or I'll pay for it, but go somewhere. Where would you like to go?

ABE: Where am I going to go? Huh? Alaska? By myself? I can't see so good, I can't walk so good. And without your Mother...

SAM: Dad.

ABE: I have nothing do you see? I have no...I have nothing.

SAM: You won't feel this way forever.

ABE: Forever, what, I'm a dead man.

SAM: Your life expectancy is, what, another ten years,/ are you just going to...?

SAM: And her life expectancy is another twenty. Don't tell me of... Stop telling me how to live my life! Stop telling me what to do from one of your textbooks! Just stop it, shut up and get away from me!

(The lights change. SAM *exits.)*

*(*ABE *eats from a can and drinks. Alone. He talks to a framed photograph.)*

ABE: Sammy came by today. It's the first Tuesday of the month so...he does that. We can't...without you to mediate, we don't...never could I suppose. It was sad. It got me thinking a lot. About the past. When I was still a Dad and not just a Father. You think he can even remember? You remember. You remember the time Sammy and I convinced you the house was haunted? He was what, six? Eight? Banging on pipes, rustling the drapes. He had you scared out of your mind. But there's no ghosts tonight. Noone to fly in through the window and brush against my cheek.

*(*ESTHER, ABE*'s dead wife, enters. She is ghostlike. Her voice is amplified, but sounds like a whisper. She carries a plate of dinner.)*

ESTHER: There are ghosts tonight.

ABE: Esther, what are you doing here?

ESTHER: You want I should go?

*(*ABE *examines her.)*

ABE: You look younger. You look beautiful. You didn't look like that.

ESTHER: I looked like this. You stopped looking. You didn't see me, you didn't see you...

ABE: I never stopped looking.

ESTHER: So you say.

(She hands the plate of food to ABE.*)*

ABE: You made brisket, you never make that anymore.

ESTHER: You had a sad day you said. So I made something special.

ABE: Did you always do that for me?

ESTHER: Of course. You missed that one too?

ABE: I love your brisket.

ESTHER: Don't get too excited, you can barely taste anything anymore. I have to add a whole container of salt to get any sort of a rise out of you.

ABE: Can I ask you something?

ESTHER: I'm going to stop you?

ABE: Are you glad you're dead?

ESTHER: Do you mean do I miss you?

ABE: I mean what I said. Don't be difficult.

ESTHER: I'm trying to clarify...

ABE: You're trying to make me sad.

ESTHER: You are sad. What do I need to try?

ABE: So you're glad?

ESTHER: I'm at peace.

ABE: Why can't you just answer a simple question?

ESTHER: I don't know, why don't you try asking me a simple question?

ABE: So you miss me?

ESTHER: Of course.

ABE: Even from there?

ESTHER: I'll never not miss you.

ABE: Because I miss you too.

ESTHER: I know.

ABE: I don't know if I can get on without you.

ESTHER: You will.

ABE: I'm not so sure.

ESTHER: God doesn't give us challenges we can't overcome.

ABE: And if He does?

ESTHER: Then we die.

ABE: And then?

ESTHER: You'll see.

ABE: I want to see. I want to see you. Will I?

ESTHER: I'm just in your mind anyway. You can do with me whatever you want. Now eat your brisket.

(He does.)

ABE: This brisket is good.

ESTHER: The memory of a thing is always better than the thing itself. *(She starts to exit.)*

ABE: Where are you going? Are you coming back?

ESTHER: I'll be back when you need me.

ABE: I always need you.

ESTHER: You might have told me while I was alive.

ABE: Didn't I? I thought I did.

(She is gone. ABE *looks at the food. From offstage we hear a scratching and a whimpering.)*

ABE: Hello?

(It continues.)

ABE: Hello? What's this? Is someone there? Another ghost?

*(*ABE *goes offstage to investigate. From where he exited, on runs* KALEF *[a dog played by a woman].* KALEF *is very happy to be inside and is energetic and hungry. She runs around a bit sniffing, panting and looking for food.* ABE *walks on after her.)*

ABE: Hold on there. You can't come in here. What are you doing? Don't go over there.

*(*ABE *shuffles around after the dog, but* KALEF *is way too fast.)*

ABE: Stop it. Stay still. Come here. Come here little doggy. Hello little doggy, come here.

*(*KALEF*'s having none of it.* ABE *goes to the table.)*

ABE: Do you want some...

(He goes to give the dog some brisket, but decides to save the brisket and offers the can. KALEF *sees the can and cautiously starts to come over to it. Sniffs it.*

ABE: Good doggy. Good dog.

*(*KALEF *is investigating the can and* ABE *starts to slowly reach to grab* KALEF*.* KALEF *doesn't notice, but at the last second rejects the can and continues running around sniffing.*

ABE: Come on. Oh. Come on. Here little poochy doggy. Alright, alright, you want the good stuff?

*(*ABE *puts the brisket on the floor.* KALEF *sees the brisket. Looks at* ABE. *This is quite an offering, the dog is impressed.* KALEF *goes to the brisket and begins to eat it ravenously.)*

ABE: You're a hungry doggy.

(While KALEF *eats,* ABE *removes her dog tag.)*

ABE: Kalef. You're a Hebrew dog. You'd think someone smart enough to be Jewish would have been smart enough to name you something other than "dog". Are you lost? *(He looks at the dog tag.)* No phone number. What am I supposed to do with you? Put up signs around the neighborhood with your picture? I have enough to do. You'll have to go.

*(*KALEF *seems to hear this and looks at* ABE *sorrowfully and whimpers.* ABE *absent mindedly puts the dog tag on the table.)*

ABE: What? You want to stay with me? You can't stay with me.

*(*KALEF *licks* ABE*'s face maniacally.)*

ABE: Alright, alright, stop it with that.

*(*KALEF *kisses* ABE*'s cheeks softly, not like a dog.)*

ABE: You're a very sweet little doggy. I'll give you some water, then you'll have to go.

*(*ABE *exits to get a bowl of water.* KALEF *looks after* ABE *sadly.* ABE *returns and sets the bowl of water on the ground.)*

ABE: Alright, you can drink this and then you have to go.

*(*KALEF *picks up the bowl and drinks it.)*

ABE: Alright, finished? Hurry up. I have no time for you.

(KALEF finishes.)

ABE: Good. Now you have to go.

(KALEF walks right up to ABE and looks him in the eye. She speaks very gently.)

KALEF: I just want to be your friend.

ABE: I know. I don't care. You have to go.

(ABE sees KALEF offstage as if she were a dinner guest.)

ABE: Good luck out there. You'll be fine. You're a very sweet little doggy. I'm sure someone will take good care of you. *(ABE returns to the table. He notices the dog tag. Calling after)* Oh. Wait. You forgot something. Kalef. Kalef, kalef, kalef.

(The lights change. Music underscores. ABE starts speaking like a much younger man.)

ABE: And that is when it happened. I felt it first inside my bones. Aches I hadn't even noticed sparked and made themselves extant, and then they slipped away right through my joints. I stood up rigidstraight for the first time in years. I felt my skin tightening and softening. I felt the follicles atop my head rejuvenate and grow. Blood cells splitting, synapse popping, penis hardening. My sight improved, the sounds came back, the hairs inside my ears just disappeared. I suddenly went from being an adjective to being a verb. I had been sullen, grumpy, and distraught, but now I'm running, climbing, soaring. My metabolism and my vigor rise. My blood runs hotter, faster, stronger. I thought I'm either dying or I'm...young. *(He looks at his reflection in the back of a spoon.)* Holy fuck. I look eighteen.

(Lights)

ABE: Suddenly it's all about: energy and speed and power. When I'd been young I didn't know I had these things. But having them again... it was overwhelming, the simple fact that suddenly I had no...fear.

(The setting begins to change.)

ABE: And so I ran. I ran and ran and ran until I just collapsed. Then I got up and danced.

(Lights and music. A club. ABE *dances wildly.)*

ABE: I danced and danced and danced. It seemed like an eternity. Time suddenly moved differently. Minutes felt like hours, they actually took longer. I had all this energy, this drive.

(Lights and music out)

ABE: So I had to have sex. Had to. When you're young, it's sometimes not an option. I went for a cocktail, I picked up a woman. I was amazed at how easy it was. Especially considering how beautiful she was. So we had sex, and yes it was...nice to have sex with such a good looking woman. But in truth I spent the time thinking about Esther (I even called her name out once) and sex without the feelings behind it, for me, as good as it felt, was just...guilt. Even now. But it worked up a mighty appetite, so I went to a diner.

*(*ABE *sits at a table and speaks to an imaginary waiter. Music out.)*

ABE: I'll have a double bacon cheeseburger deluxe, a side of onion rings, and a chocolate milkshake. And an order of macaroni and cheese. I wanted to tell someone of my conquest, share my victory with a friend. But I had no friends, young or old. All I had were memories that reached back long before the years of my body. That's not youth.

*(*JUNIOR *enters with a stickball bat and sits with* ABE.*)*

JUNIOR: Hey, where were you? We missed you on the street.

ABE: You win?

JUNIOR: Of course we won.

ABE: Without me?

JUNIOR: You're not the only hitter we got.

ABE: Yeah, who else?

JUNIOR: Me.

ABE: You? Please.

JUNIOR: Yeah, me. Check this out.

(He hands him a baseball card.)

ABE: No way. Where'd you get that?

JUNIOR: I bet DeSilva I'd hit his next pitch past the third light.

ABE: You hit DeSilva past the third light?

JUNIOR: Yep.

ABE: Junior, you did not.

JUNIOR: Did too.

ABE: Every time you lie your eyes cross like Mister Mandelbaum's.

JUNIOR: Alright, Brody hit it. But I made the bet so I got the card.

ABE: What did you bet?

JUNIOR: A date with my sister.

ABE: You can't bet that.

JUNIOR: Why not? There was no way Brody was going to let DeSilva go out with my Sister.

ABE: Good point.

JUNIOR: So where were you?

ABE: I don't have to tell you where I was. You are not the boss of me.

JUNIOR: You were with Esther.

ABE: So what if I was?

JUNIOR: Again? Why don't you just marry her?

ABE: You know what Junior? I just might do that.

*(*JUNIOR *starts to run off.)*

JUNIOR: Abe loves Esther, Abe loves Esther.

ABE: Junior.

*(*JUNIOR *stops and turns around. He acts older.)*

JUNIOR: Yeah?

ABE: How old were you when you died?

JUNIOR: Thirty-fvie.

ABE: You were a kid to me.

JUNIOR: Always will be.

ABE: And DeSilva? And Brody?

JUNIOR: They made it longer. But now we're all gone. Just you is left.

ABE: Why can't we all die in order like we're supposed to?

JUNIOR: Life isn't that kind.

ABE: Do you see them? On the other side?

JUNIOR: You might as well believe I do.

ABE: Why's that?

JUNIOR: Because if you're wrong, you'll never know it.

ABE: But I want to know.

JUNIOR: You'll know all in good time. For now, just make good use of the time you've got back.

*(*JUNIOR *exits as* SAM *enters along with two chairs.* SAM *and* ABE *each sit.)*

SAM: So what brings you to see me?

ABE: Something sad happened to me.

SAM: Can you tell me what that was?

ABE: Someone close to me died.

SAM: I'm sorry. Who?

ABE: My... My Mother.

SAM: I'm sorry. How did she die?

ABE: She was old. Old people die.

SAM: Yes they do. Was it sudden?

ABE: Yes.

SAM: I'm sorry. That sounds very difficult. And this is something you want to talk about with me?

ABE: It is. Yes, it is. Did anyone close to you ever die?

SAM: We're not talking about me.

ABE: You don't want to tell me?

SAM: We're here to talk about you.

ABE: I take that as a no then.

SAM: Take it however you like. Why do you feel it's important to take it as a no?

ABE: Is that how this works, you just ask me a bunch of questions?

SAM: That's part of it. Does that bother you? Sorry. If you talk then I don't have to ask questions.

ABE: What do you want me to talk about?

SAM: Why don't you tell me how you think your Mother's death is affecting you.

ABE: How is your Mother's death affecting you?

SAM: What makes you think my Mother is dead?

ABE: If my Mother was old, your Mother must be... very old.

SAM: Tell me about you and your Mother.

ABE: Alright. I miss her. I loved her very much. My Father's still alive but I don't love him nearly as much. Even though he loves me. He loves me more than anything. I'm all he has left. And there's nothing on this earth stronger than family. Even I know that.

SAM: Go on.

ABE: When I was a kid he and I used to do all sorts of stuff. Play ball, stick ball, he taught me how to build ships in a bottle, he made me laugh, and then somehow we just...

SAM: What?

ABE: Grew up. He um, he wrote this poem for me. *(He takes a very old and worn piece of paper out of his wallet.)*

SAM: He wrote you a poem? That's very...caring.

ABE: Yeah. He wrote it for me on my first birthday. And then he...he carried it with him, for years and years. It goes like this: *(He reads from the paper, but knows it by heart:)* This year has been a gift from heaven sent
Because, my son, your style beguiles me
I thought I knew what my existence meant,
but life would just be strife without your smiles. See
this year has been a whirlwind, full of fun
I saw you sit, I saw you stand, I saw you walk
We hugged and kissed and once I wiped your bum.
I heard you cry, I heard you laugh, I heard you talk.
Now all that I can think of is your future, son.
Life's path conceals and then reveals it's knowledge
Will you stay this loving to me? Will you stay this fun?

Maybe one day you will go to college.
Whatever you become, we'll never be apart,
Because your smiles fire fuels my hardened heart.

SAM: That's very beautiful. You're very lucky to have such a caring and articulate Father. Not everyone has that.

ABE: Some people have it but they don't know it.

SAM: I suppose that's true. But if you don't know it, then it's as good as not there. It's when something goes unsaid, when you don't express your...

ABE: I tried Sam, I tried.

SAM: Tried what?

ABE: Life just...gets away from you. The hands of time have a way of beating you into submission.

SAM: What exactly are you...?

ABE: I'm just a fucking human being. I shouldn't have come here.

*(*ABE *exits the scene.* SAM *exits as do the chairs.)*

ABE: I ran. And ran and ran. I wanted to run faster.
So I did what I should have done a long, long time ago.

(A car salesperson, DANA, *enters.)*

DANA: The Porsche nine-twenty-one Carrera convertible is the most elegant Porsche ever.

ABE: How much?

DANA: Intensive development work has given this car a new level of aerodynamic refinement making it the most aerodynamically efficient convertible in the world.

ABE: How much?

DANA: The improved aerodynamics are manifested in low noise levels inside the car, low fuel consumption, superb performance and safe handling even at high speeds.

ABE: Safe handling at high speeds. How much?

*(*DANA *shows* ABE *a slip of paper.)*

ABE: Holy fuck.

*(*DANA *exits.)*

ABE: It basically was every penny that I had. But who cares? You only live once right? Or. Well you know what I mean. Seize the day. What the heck, this whole second chance was like getting..., like getting a second a chance. I'm young. I do what I want. I bought it.

(Lights and sound. He's driving the car.)

ABE: And so I'm riding down the streets of New York City in my Porsche and I admit I'm going way too fast, but that's the point. And suddenly I close my eyes and scream: "Esther I love you! Sam I love you! I love my beautiful family!"

(The sound of a nasty pile-up)

INTERLUDE 1: THE POLICE STATION

*(*MARLENE *sits at the table rubbing her temples.* ABE, JONTHAN *and* CATHY *sit cross legged on the table as before.* DON *appears in the doorway.)*

DON: Sorry.

MARLENE: Hey.

DON: The accident?

MARLENE: The car?

DON: Our witness...?

MARLENE: Yeah?

DON: He says...?

MARLENE: Yeah?

DON: The driver...?

MARLENE: Yeah?

DON: Eighteen or so.

MARLENE: And?

DON: He's sixty.

MARLENE: He didn't see, happened fast.

DON: No.

MARLENE: No?

DON: Weirder than that.

MARLENE: How so?

DON: Don't know.

MARLENE: But...

DON: Something's weird.

MARLENE: He'll talk. They always do.

DON: You never do.

MARLENE: What?

DON: Talk.

MARLENE: No.

(Pause)

DON: They're still questioning him.

MARLENE: Keep me...

DON: posted?

MARLENE: Yeah.

DON: Will do.

(DON *doesn't leave.* MARLENE *notices.)*

MARLENE: What?

DON: I want to know her story though.

MARLENE: Who?

DON: The woman.

MARLENE: Who got hit?

DON: Yeah.

MARLENE: Why?

DON: Something about her.

MARLENE: Yeah?

DON: Something behind her eyes.

MARLENE: Yeah?

(DON *exits.)*

*(*ABE, JONTHAN *and* CATHY *look at each other, a tad confused.)*

(JONTHAN *and* ABE *turn to* CATHY.*)*

(A spotlight hits CAHTY. As she speaks the others exit as the stage is set for:)

SECTION 2: CATHY'S LIVING ROOM, A C D STORE, A PARK

CATHY: Ok, I'm also not going to begin with a start, but with an end, but first let me say this: the thing that I hate the most is the lie, and I'm not talking about when you tell someone something that isn't true, I'm talking about when you look into someone's eyes and you see the potential, you see the soul inside the person, and you decide not to let it out, you hide inside yourself. To me that's a lie. And it's hateful.

(The lights change. CATHY *and* EVAN, *her husband, sit in their living room and discuss.)*

EVAN: Well, it's Wednesday.

CATHY: I know.

EVAN: So, what do you think?

CATHY: What do you think?

EVAN: I asked you first.

CATHY: I think it sort of worked.

EVAN: No you don't.

CATHY: It didn't work. So what do we do?

EVAN: What else can we / do?

CATHY: You're really ready to throw this away after seven years?

EVAN: ...

CATHY: Wow. *(She breaks down a bit.)*

EVAN: O K, O K, come on, I'm sorry.

(They hug.)

CATHY: It's not exactly like you're Mister Emotionally Available. You don't meet all my needs either.

EVAN: I'm aware of that.

CATHY: But I don't see how today became some magic deadline. If we want to keep fighting to stay together, we should do that.

EVAN: We're not happy together. We grew apart.

CATHY: We grew up. Is that a crime?

EVAN: I don't want to grow up.

CATHY: Nobody WANTS to grow up. You have to grow up.

EVAN: You make me feel old. Settled.

CATHY: I don't MAKE you feel anything.

EVAN: Well, I feel those things.

CATHY: Yeah. Time'll do that.

EVAN: You don't exactly help. You never want to do anything anymore. We just sit around all the time and do nothing.

CATHY: Welcome to life. You slow down. You can't recapture your youth.

EVAN: If I'd never lost it I wouldn't have to / recapture it.

CATHY: You think I took it from you?

EVAN: I don't think you tried to stop it.

CATHY: It's not stoppable.

EVAN: You can try. I tried.

CATHY: How?

EVAN: You know how.

CATHY: What? Evan, cheating on your wife does not make you young. It makes you an asshole.

EVAN: So if I'm an asshole why did you stay with me?

CATHY: We're married.

EVAN: But I betrayed you.

CATHY: And I got over it.

EVAN: How?

CATHY: How? How?

EVAN: Yeah, how?

CATHY: Because I guess I don't blame you.

EVAN: —!?

CATHY: If I was married to me I'd cheat too. I'd find some gorgeous babe and fuck her. I mean who wants to look at this all the time?

EVAN: So you forgave me.

CATHY: Aren't we past all this?

EVAN: Maybe if you hadn't forgiven me, maybe if you'd held it against me and made me pay for it, maybe we wouldn't be splitting up.

CATHY: I...I have no response to that.

EVAN: You mad at me?

CATHY: No.

EVAN: Yes you are.

CATHY: Fine, I am.

EVAN: So tell me. Yell at me, tell me to fuck off.

CATHY: What good would that do?

EVAN: Might make you feel better.

CATHY: No thanks.

EVAN: Why not?

CATHY: I don't want to fight with you.

EVAN: Why not? Go ahead.

CATHY: I don't want to.

EVAN: Yell at me.

CATHY: No.

EVAN: What are you afraid of?

CATHY: Nothing.

EVAN: What? Tell me.

CATHY: I'm... I'm afraid you'll leave. I'm afraid you'll leave and never come back. I thought we loved each other.

EVAN: We do.

CATHY: Why did you fall in love with me?

EVAN: I don't know, it just happened.

CATHY: But can you remember? One thing? That you loved about me?

EVAN: There are many things that I love about you.

CATHY: Name one.

EVAN: They're not namable. You get to a point where it's just...everything.

CATHY: Everything? And when every thing becomes everything it becomes nothing.

EVAN: Maybe.

CATHY: You know when my Dad left my Mom, he told her she'd never find another man. That she was worthless and pathetic. I always thought we would last forever but that if we didn't we would end in a big blowout too.

EVAN: So have a blowout.

CATHY: You're the one who's supposed to have the blowout. It's not fair of you to keep loving me.

EVAN: I don't know what you want me to say.

CATHY: I want you to say we'll keep trying.

EVAN: I can't say that.

CATHY: Then I want you to say goodbye.

*(*EVAN *exits.* DANA *enters and paints* CATHY*'s toes, or makes sundaes, or otherwise tends to her.* CATHY *eats popcorn or other junk food throughout.)*

DANA: He was no good anyway.

CATHY: He isn't dead, you can speak about him in the present tense.

DANA: He is no good anyway.

CATHY: He isn't?

DANA: No! He's totally... He's such a...O K, he is. He's pretty great.

CATHY: Are you trying to make me feel better?

DANA: Well...have you really done everything you could?

CATHY: Yes! I fought so hard to keep this marriage together it's ridiculous. But now he's done fighting. He's giving up.

DANA: What did your Mom say?

CATHY: She cried. She was as supportive as she could be.

DANA: Have you told your Dad?

CATHY: No.

DANA: He's going to flip isn't he?

CATHY: He's going to worse than flip. Do you know that Evan and I lived together for two years before we got married and he never knew.

DANA: No!?

CATHY: He wouldn't have...he couldn't....

DANA: How did he not find out?

CATHY: Noone told him.

DANA: He never called you?

CATHY: Nope.

DANA: In two years?!

CATHY: Nope. I always called him.

DANA: That is insane.

(Pause)

CATHY: Dana, what am I going to do?

DANA: Can you kill him?

CATHY: What?

DANA: I mean, you know, not you personally, but like...have him killed.

CATHY: Seriously.

DANA: Seriously? Oh, seriously. Well. You're going to cry your eyes out, you're gonna feel like shit, if you were me, you'd get VERY drunk. A lot. But you're not me, you're you, so you'll eat tons of ice cream, and eventually you'll meet someone else.

CATHY: No. I was lucky to get Evan. I mean, look at me.

DANA: What's wrong with you?

CATHY: Dana?

DANA: What?

CATHY: I'm ugly.

DANA: Shut the fuck up. What the hell do you want to look like? Some stick with tits? I'm so sick of hearing that. It's ridiculous.

CATHY: Don't be nice.

DANA: You're beautiful. Fuck Cosmo.

CATHY: But what do you think it's like for the really beautiful?

DANA: Jennifer Lopez is not any happier than we are.

CATHY: ...

DANA: OK, maybe a little happier. But I still think she's skanky.

CATHY: I feel like such a loser.

DANA: You're not a / loser.

CATHY: How could I not? We failed. I lose.

DANA: Don't torture yourself. You don't know where this will lead.

CATHY: I don't think it'll lead somewhere good.

DANA: Do you know that parable?

CATHY: Which one?

DANA: I don't know, it's like Chinese or something and, I don't remember it that well, but you know...like this Chinese farmer loses his horse and that's like really bad, cause, I don't know, he like really needs his horse or whatever, but then the horse returns and is like carrying the farmer's long lost son or something so he's totally psyched, but then like the son has some disease and the whole family gets it so that sucks, but then like because they're all inside and sick they miss this insane hurricane or something...

CATHY: Are you making this up?

DANA: No. It's a parable. It just means you don't know what's good and what's bad. You don't know what'll lead to what.

CATHY: Sometimes you know.

DANA: You don't. You never know. At least it's not going to be one of those messy divorces right?

CATHY: No. He doesn't care. He doesn't want anything except his stupid jazz collection.

DANA: See?

CATHY: He doesn't want anything except to never see me again.

DANA: Oh Cath.

CATHY: What did I do that was so wrong? He doesn't even look at me anymore. He goes whole days without even noticing me. I'm worthless. I'm nothing. I hate myself. I'm so scared.

DANA: I hate it when you talk like that.

CATHY: Can I not mourn the death of my marriage?

DANA: If that's what you want.

CATHY: I want him to see me.

DANA: It's going to work out.

CATHY: You don't know that.

DANA: Look at me. It's going to work out.

CATHY: Look, I don't need platitude advice from someone who's never had a relationship that lasted more than three months and whose most intimate relationship is with a sloberry dog named "Woofer".

DANA: *(Upset)* O K.

CATHY: Oh God, Dana, I'm so sorry.

DANA: No, it's fine. You're right. Advice is bullshit.

CATHY: I'm sorry. I didn't... I shouldn't have said yes to you coming over here. I just I'm not ready to deal yet.

DANA: Clearly.

(Lights change. DANA *exits.)*

CATHY: Fuck. Fuck, fuck, fuck, fuck, fuck.

(There is a scratch at the door.)

CATHY: Go away.

(It persists.)

CATHY: Dana I don't want to talk to anyone. I'm sorry. I won't be myself right now. I'll call you tomorrow O K?

(It persists and increases.)

CATHY: I'm not in the mood. You could call first you know O K?

(More)

CATHY: Leave me alone. Just leave me alone.

(Scratching scratching scratching. CATHY *exits to the door.)*

CATHY: Fine. I'm coming. What do you want?

(From where she exited on runs KALEF *the dog.* CATHY *chases her a bit, but* KALEF *eludes her.)*

CATHY: Hey. What are you doing? Look at you, you're so cute. Are you lost? Come here, let me see you.

*(*KALEF *stands, wary but curious.)*

CATHY: What kind of dog are you? I've never seen a dog like you. You're so sweet. Come here.

(She holds out her hand for KALEF *to sniff.* KALEF *cautiously approaches and smells.* CATHY *pets her.)*

CATHY: Hello little doggy face. Yes, you're a good dog aren't you?

*(*CATHY *pets* KALEF *until they both calm down.* CATHY *looks at the dog tags.*

CATHY: Are you lost? How did you get in here? There's no dogs in this building. Kalef. That's a weird name for a dog. No phone number? Are you hungry? Thirsty? *(She examines her junk food.)* I don't think you want any of this. Let me see what else I have.

*(*CATHY *exits.* KALEF *sniffs the food. She sits down and starts eating popcorn like someone at the movies)*

CATHY: *(O S)* I don't really have very much.
(She re-enters.) Hey. No. Don't eat that.

*(*CATHY *snatches the popcorn.* KALEF *looks at her like she has two heads.)*

CATHY: Oh My God, you are the cutest dog. What am I going to do with you? I can't keep you, they don't allow doggies in this building.

*(*KALEF *rolls onto her back.)*

CATHY: You want me to scratch your belly? Come here.

(She scratches KALEF*'s belly which makes* KALEF *happy which makes* CATHY *happy.)*

CATHY: A-rough-rough-rough you're so cute.
Arough-rough-rough. Yes little doggy doggy
doggy rough-rough-rough.

*(*KALEF *jumps up stretches and lays down.)*

CATHY: Are you sleepy? You can't stay here.
My super would freak.

*(*KALEF *yawns. She looks at* CATHY *longingly.)*

KALEF: But I make you so happy.

CATHY: Oh alright. But just for tonight. Tomorrow I'm taking you to out to get you adopted.

*(*KALEF *jumps up and down, happy, then kisses* CATHY *on the cheek over and over.)*

CATHY: O K, O K, you're welcome, you're welcome.

*(*KALEF *lays down to go to sleep.* CATHY *looks at her. After a bit,* CATHY *lays down and curls up with her so they are spooning. They relax and sleep. They both seem very peaceful and happy. The lights fade on them.)*

(After a bit the lights fade up again. It is morning. CATHY *is in the same position but* KALEF *is gone.)*

CATHY: Hey. Doggy? *(She searches around looking for the dog.)* Little doggy? Kalef? Kalef? Hello? Are you hiding? Where did you go? You couldn't have gotten out of here. Where are you? Did I dream you? *(She finds the dog tag.)* Kalef. Kalef kalef kalef. That is so weird.

(She exits off. We hear the sound of bathroom noises. Suddenly she screams.)

CATHY: Oh my God! What the Fucking Fuck!?
(She rushes onstage and addresses the audience.)
I cannot possibly explain this to you, I was wiping the sleep from my eyes, and I look in the mirror, and I was beautiful, I mean gorgeous, I mean not like some good hair day kind of a thing, I was a totally different person (except for my eyes, I didn't even recognize myself). My voice was different because, I guess, my body was different; physiologically different from my hairless toes, to my longer legs, to my wider hips and bigger breasts, to higher cheekbones, to, Jesus Fucking Christ! *(She runs offstage. Screams. Runs back on.)* I'm not kidding, I'm gorgeous, so of course the first thing I did was drink, tequila is very good for situations like these (not that I've ever been in a situation remotely like this) then I washed it down with some orange juice so it seemed more like breakfast. Having come to peace with the fact that I was completely not at peace with this but it was nonetheless true, the next thing I did was run out to get some new clothes, you know, something that would flatter the new me more, but when I stepped outside it was like I was stepping into a different country: people holding doors for me, smiling at me, telling me to have a good day. I asked a cop, just to make sure this was still New York and he looked at me like I was crazy, but he didn't care, he couldn't stop staring at me, I mean who knew that the beautiful had it like this? Do they even notice or do they just take it for granted? I was walking differently, talking

differently, the world treats you differently and you become different and so of course the first thing I had to do was have sex. I figured I'd go to a bar that night and see if anyone talked to me, I felt like I had all the power in the world but I should take my time, take my pick, wait for my pitch, but I didn't want to wait, I wanted to feel a man on top of me, I wanted to be with someone who was dying to be there, not laying there out of obligation, So I found some guy, and took him home and you want to know the truth? I was more nervous than he was, I mean it's been a long time since I've been with anyone besides Evan, and I may be different on the outside but I'm still Chatty Cathy in here, so anyway, I brought him home and he was in ecstasy but you know what? I had done the same thing I always do, but I guess with these tits and these legs, it was heaven for him. Although he did call me Esther once. But really, I didn't mind, I mean Esther's as good a name for the new me as any at this point and for me there was something exciting about the pure carnal pleasure of lustful sex that had absolutely no baggage attached.

(The setting begins to change.)

CATHY: But still. There was only one man I really wanted to have sex with. So I went to visit him at his used cd store.

(She walks up to EVAN *in the store. She puts on the sexy. Which may or may not be such a great idea.)*

CATHY: Excuse me.

EVAN: What can I do for you?

CATHY: Um. You know that song? It's a swing song I guess. It's like all these drums and then like *(She sings the opening of Sing-Sing-Sing as best she can which is not necessarily very well).*

EVAN: Sing Sing Sing.

CATHY: That's it.

EVAN: Benny Goodman.

CATHY: Right. Isn't there like some famous recording of it live?

EVAN: Carnegie hall. 1937. Sure. Hang on. Here you go. *(He produces the C D.)*

CATHY: Is it good?

EVAN: Do you like Swing music?

CATHY: I like that song.

EVAN: Well if you're looking for more of an introduction I'd recommend this one. More of a compilation.

(He gives her a different disc.)

CATHY: Maybe I'll take them both.

EVAN: Can't hurt. Is that it?

(CATHY giggles.)

EVAN: What?

CATHY: No, I don't know, I just have flutters in my stomach.

EVAN: Hmmm. Well, twenty four ninety eight.

(Lights. CATHY addresses the audience.)

CATHY: Well I had to give him credit, he certainly wasn't trying to make it with anything that moved but still I was kind of hurt he hadn't fallen for my allure so the next day I went back.

(Lights)

CATHY: Hi, I don't know if you remember me.

EVAN: Sing Sing Sing.

CATHY: Yeah. It was great. They both were. What else could you recommend?

EVAN: Well, there's Glen Miller, Tommy Dorsey, Arty Shaw. Which of the tracks on the compilation did you like most?

CATHY: Which one do you like?

EVAN: Well, personally my favorite is Count Bassie. There's a live recording of him at Newport. When Joe Willimas comes on in the last set... / heaven.

CATHY: *(Overlapping)* Heaven?

EVAN: Yeah.

CATHY: How did I guess? OK sold.

EVAN: Will that be it?

CATHY: You know I didn't really come here to buy C Ds.

EVAN: Well that's all we have. That why we're called "Just C Ds".

CATHY: No, I...What are you doing tonight?

EVAN: You're asking me out? Look, I...

CATHY: You're married?

EVAN: Sort of.

CATHY: That's enough of an opening for me.

EVAN: I don't think I should.

CATHY: Come on, you can beguile me with your knowledge of Count Bassie.

EVAN: That is tough to pass up.

CATHY: Do you like Sushi?

EVAN: I am a big sushi fan.

CATHY: How did I guess? Bassie, Sushi and...a walk through the park? Who gets hurt?

EVAN: Alright you're on.

(A little theatre magic and we're in the park.)

CATHY: So tell me about your "sort of" wife.

EVAN: What would you like to know?

CATHY: Start with the "sort of" part.

EVAN: We're separated, getting a divorce, probably.

CATHY: And the wife part?

EVAN: She's great.

CATHY: But...?

EVAN: But she just doesn't seem to care anymore.

CATHY: About?

EVAN: Anything. There's no passion. She's happy just being settled and staid. She wants me to change all the time. Hell, she knew who I was when she married me. I just want to be who I am you know?

CATHY: So then why get married in the first place if not to grow together and make each other better?

EVAN: You're taking her side?

CATHY: I'm not taking a side. But they do call it settling down.

EVAN: You get married to be with someone forever.

CATHY: And then?

EVAN: And then you realize that forever is a long time.

CATHY: How long have you been married?

EVAN: Seven years.

CATHY: That's not so long. Maybe it was the seven year itch.

EVAN: No. We just grew apart.

CATHY: How do you avoid that? Two different people. Is it inevitable?

EVAN: Maybe. I don't know. I'm certainly not the expert.

CATHY: I'm sorry if I'm prying.

EVAN: It's ok. It feels good to talk about it without all the...

CATHY: What?

EVAN: Bullshit. Anger. Baggage.

CATHY: So if you could be honest with her, and without all the bullshit, anger, baggage, what would you say?

EVAN: I don't know.

CATHY: Come on.

(He thinks about it then looks right in CATHY*'s eyes.)*

EVAN: I'd tell her that she doesn't understand what an amazing person she is but if she did, she'd be that much more amazing. If she could have just seen herself through my eyes and trusted that. I'd tell her how beautiful she is inside and out. Just because I didn't always know how to express that to her doesn't make it not true. And I'd tell her that just because we didn't work out, doesn't mean anything bad about her.

CATHY: Do you know who I am?

EVAN: Who?

CATHY: No. I mean. Forget it. Inside joke. So... if you love her so much why couldn't you express it to her?

EVAN: Why? Because I'm a fucking human being. No, worse, I'm a man. Why did you ask me out?

CATHY: What do you mean?

EVAN: Well you're obviously very beautiful. Confident. What made you want to go out with me?

CATHY: You think I'm beautiful?

EVAN: I don't think I'm the first to tell you.

CATHY: No, but that doesn't mean it doesn't feel good to hear it. From you. You looked like someone who would have something interesting to say.

EVAN: Hmm. What does that mean?

CATHY: It means shut up and kiss me.

(He does. The lights change. He exits. She addresses the audience.)

CATHY: Having sex with your soon to be ex-husband, with him thinking you're a totally different and much better looking person; now there's one to fuck with your head. It was like we were having sex for the first time which I suppose in a way we were but I was used to him, his body, his kisses, his... but he was kissing me differently, like he didn't know what to expect, there was passion. Promise. Hope. I just wanted to cry and tell him who I was, but...I couldn't and then when we were done, laying there in our post coital bliss, he looked at me and said: "you have beautiful eyes". Of all the things he could have said. The next morning I had an overwhelming desire to clean his apartment, but instead I thanked him, kissed him and left.
I decided to walk home and try to clear my head.
Part of me wanted to just seduce him and stay with him but the rest thought I was out of my mind, I mean could I really live that lie? But then again, with this new body I'd have to reinvent myself anyway so why not? Now I had a chance to do it again and get it right because he could see me in here, see through my eyes, I know he could. So I stepped out of his new building and walked for what seemed like days. I don't know, maybe it was. I closed my eyes and screamed, "Evan loves me! I love me."

(The same sound of the pile up)

INTERLUDE 2:
THE POLICE ROOM

(The police station. MARLENE *sits at the table rubbing her temples.* ABE, JONATHAN *and* CATHY *sit cross legged o the table as before.* DON *appears in the doorway.)*

DON: Ready?

MARLENE: Car accident?

DON: Yup.

MARLENE: Hit me.

DON: Our witness...?

MARLENE: Yeah?

DON: *(Making quotes with his fingers)* "The woman's gorgeous. GORGEOUS."

MARLENE: So?

DON: "Couldn't take his eyes off her."

MARLENE: So?

DON: "Doesn't blame the guy for losing control of the Porsche."

MARLENE: You said there was something about her.

DON: *(He throws her photo on the desk)* Behind the eyes. She's O K. Nothing to write home about. Different strokes.

MARLENE: Yup.

DON: Wishes he'd saved her.

MARLENE: Wishing's useless.

DON: Yeah?

MARLENE: Pisses me off.

DON: What?

MARLENE: Empty wishes.

DON: Why?

MARLENE: What?

DON: Why?

MARLENE: Nothing. Sorry.

DON: No prob.

(Pause)

MARLENE: Still interrogating?

DON: Witness? Yup.

MARLENE: Can't wait.

DON: For?

MARLENE: His description.

DON: The naked guy?

MARLENE: Why naked?

DON: Why naked? Why naked? Don't know. Don't know. *(He exits.)*

*(*ABE, JONTHAN *and* CATHY *look at each other, a tad confused.* CATHY *and* ABE *turn to* JONTHAN.*)*

(A spotlight hits JONTHAN. *As he speaks the others exit as the stage is set for:)*

SECTION 3: AN OFFICE, JONTHAN'S APARTMENT, A DOG RUN, A PHARMACY, DANA'S APARTMENT

JONATHAN: You know what I'll do?
And I know this sounds crazy,

but I'll start at a start
and not start at an end.
It's...
Radical
I know.
Just let me get dressed,
Before I express,
I'll explain the whole
"naked thing"
in a minute.
(He starts dressing.)
But
before I start
With my start
let me just say one thing:
When you can't
deal with
another person?
It's very hard.
I grant you.
Be it a lover,
a parent,
a child,
whatever.
I'm sorry for you.
I am.
It sucks.
And when you can't deal with yourself?
well O K,
there's no escaping yourself,
so that's a tough one.
I feel bad.
I do.
It sucks.
But when you
can't
deal

with society?
that leaves you in a whole other
Kettle of ballgames.
Because it
always
seems like there's a way out.
A way to be somewhere without
actually?
having to be there.
A way to be someone without
actually?
having to be him.
But in reality?
it's just
not
possible.
Now don't get me wrong,
I love America.
Freedom,
liberty,
and the pursuit of material wealth.
I'm all for it.
I just
don't like
dealing
with other people.
Why?
...
WellifIknewthat,IguessIwouldn'tbeafuckinghumanbeing

(JONTHAN's *apartment.* CYNTHIA, JONTHAN's *mother, is folding his laundry.)*

CYNTHIA: How old are you?

JONATHAN: You know how old I am.

CYNTHIA: Thirty-five. Which means?

JONATHAN: I'm old enough to take care of myself?

CYNTHIA: Wrong. I wish. It means you should be married. With kids by now.

JONATHAN: Leave me alone.

CYNTHIA: I'd like to see a Grandchild before I die.

JONATHAN: ...

CYNTHIA: And making a decent living. What are these jobs? I paid all that money for you to learn about computers, why can't you get a job doing that?

JONATHAN: Right.

CYNTHIA: What do you do? Write poetry all day?

JONATHAN: Yup.

CYNTHIA: And why haven't you found a nice girl?

JONATHAN: I don't know.

CYNTHIA: You're not gay are you?

JONATHAN: Nope.

CYNTHIA: Are you sure?

JONATHAN: And if I was?

CYNTHIA: It would be fine. But you're not right? So what's the problem?

JONATHAN: I just haven't found / anyone I think...

CYNTHIA: There's noone at work?

JONATHAN: It's me and one other guy.

CYNTHIA: Well, do you go out? Maybe a hobby could help you find someone. You want me to take out a personal ad for you? Or do it on the computer, I read everyone's doing it on the computer. You can't be so shy all the time.

JONATHAN: Sorry.

CYNTHIA: Don't apologize. Do something about it.

JONATHAN: OK, I'll try.

CYNTHIA: That's what you say, but you don't do it.

JONATHAN: I'll do it.

CYNTHIA: When?

JONATHAN: I don't know. Soon? Tomorrow?

CYNTHIA: No you won't. You can't even call your Mother, how are you going to find a wife?

JONATHAN: I'm not in a hurry.

CYNTHIA: You're thirty-five.

JONATHAN: So?

CYNTHIA: So it's time already...

JONATHAN: O K.

CYNTHIA: ...you just have to put your mind to it.

JONATHAN: Fine.

CYNTHIA: So you'll try?

JONATHAN: Yup.

CYNTHIA: Good. Thank you. Your poor old Mother appreciates it. Just try. That's all I want from you alright?

JONATHAN: Sure. My therapist says / I should...

CYNTHIA: You're in therapy?

JONATHAN: Uh...yeah.

CYNTHIA: Why? You're not sick. You don't need therapy.

JONATHAN: Um, O K.

CYNTHIA: If you need someone to talk to, you can talk to me.

JONATHAN: Oh. O K. Yeah, great.

CYNTHIA: Oh by the way, I enrolled you in a Klezmer dance class.

JONATHAN: What?

CYNTHIA: Klezmer it's a...

JONATHAN: I know what it is.

CYNTHIA: It's at the 92nd St Y. It looks very interesting. You're going to love it.

JONATHAN: I really don't / want that.

CYNTHIA: How do you know if you don't try?

JONATHAN: I...I'll..., O K I'll...thanks. That's great.

CYNTHIA: See that? And look, your laundry's done.

JONATHAN: What?

CYNTHIA: Your laundry. So now let's see about that kitchen.

(CYNTHIA exits and the setting changes as JONTHAN addresses the audience.)

JONATHAN: Needless to say: I didn't take the class. And needless to say: I didn't find a wife. But do something about my job? I did something about my job.

(JONTHAN and EVAN stand behind the counter of the C D store.)

JONTHAN: I have to quit....

EVAN: That's cool.

JONATHAN: ...I'm sorry, I know you'll be...what? You could sound a little sad.

EVAN: Oh, ok. I'm sorry. I'm really sorry. I'm really sad.

JONATHAN: Are you ok?

EVAN: No. Yeah. I had an amazing night last night. I slept with the most beautiful woman I've ever seen.

JONATHAN: I thought that was your wife.

EVAN: It is. I think it was.

JONATHAN: I thought you two were splitting up.

EVAN: We are.

JONATHAN: So you slept with her?

EVAN: I think I did.

JONATHAN: Well I'm no expert, but that sounds pretty dumb.

EVAN: I told the truth. I expressed myself. I opened up.

JONATHAN: Look, could you just mail my last check to me? I gotta go.

EVAN: What? Yeah, sure.

JONATHAN: What are you going to do?

EVAN: I'm going to call my wife. *(He exits.)*

*(*SAMPSON *sits behind his desk.* JONTHAN *sits in a chair.)*

SAMPSON: Are you sure you want this job?

JONATHAN: Yup.

SAMPSON: You're really overqualified.

JONATHAN: Yup.

SAMPSON: And you understand that if you don't stay two years, your / options don't...

JONATHAN: I read the contract. I don't have any... whatever, problems.

SAMPSON: So why would you want this job?

JONATHAN: Why? Well. I like the idea of working out of my house. I can develop your sites, email you paperwork, you can check my work on the web. There won't be a whole lot of...face to face interaction.

SAMPSON: No, there won't.

JONATHAN: That's worth a lot to me.

SAMPSON: But you could get a / much more...

JONATHAN: It's worth a lot to me.

SAMPSON: Well. Alright then. You're hired. Congratulations.

(Lights. Time passes. The setting changes to JONTHAN*'s apartment.* JONTHAN *is on the phone.)*

JONATHAN: Hi Szechuan East? Hi. Look. I'd like to make an... uh, arrangement ok? This'll be like an ongoing credit card order ok? Yeah, like an account, that's right. Each night at sevent-thirty bring me a D7 with white rice, fried dumplings and a coke ok. The address is 231 Mott 5D. Just leave it outside the door, O K? no need to ring the bell. Yes, each night same thing. Add a three dollar tip for the guy and if it's like raining or snowing or something make it five. Oh, and don't be late ever K? Thanks.

(He hangs up. There is a scratch at the door. JONTHAN *goes back into the scene.)*

JONATHAN: Just leave it outside the door, what are you new?

(More scratching)

JONATHAN: It's paid for, don't worry about it.

(You won't be surprised to learn that the scratching continues.)

JONATHAN: Jesus Fucking Christ. What is it?

*(*JONTHAN *goes offstage.* KALEF *runs on carrying a bag of Chinese food.)*

JONATHAN: What the fuck? They've got dog delivery people now? Gimme that.

(JONTHAN *goes after the bag but* KALEF *evades him.)*

JONATHAN: Gimme my food. Gimme it. Gimme. I'm calling the restaurant.

(JONTHAN *picks up the phone. Turns his back on* KALEF. *While he talks,* KALEF *takes out some dumplings and starts eating them.)*

JONATHAN: Hi, yeah, this is the guy at 231 Mott, 5D, you send my order every night? Right Mister D7, so what's with the dog? The dog. You got dogs delivering food now? What is that? What is he, faster than a guy on a bike? Well, he won't give me my food. You want to talk to him please and tell him to give me my damn food? Hang on.

(He turns around. Sees KALEF *eating.)*

JONATHAN: Hey, what are you doing? Those are my dumplings.

(He throws down the phone and goes after the dog.)

JONATHAN: Gimme those.

(JONTHAN *chases* KALEF. KALEF *seems to be enjoying it, like a teenage girl who finally has the attention of the boy of her dreams. Finally* JONTHAN *catches her and wrestles with her, he gets the food. This makes him feel triumphant, almost like a film noir detective.)*

JONATHAN: Ha-ha. Enough of that. Alright, tell me who sent you. What do you want? What's the big idea?

(KALEF *looks at him flirtatiously.)*

JONATHAN: Give up the goods and I'll give you a dumpling.

(KALEF *comes over to* JONTHAN *and kisses him seductively.* JONTHAN *gives her a dumpling.)*

JONATHAN: That's better.

(He opens the bag and takes out the food. They sit down together and eat silently but humanly like boyfriend and girlfriend.)

(Lights change. KALEF *clears the table as* JONTHAN *calls after her.)*

JONATHAN: I think I'm in love with you. I mean, not sexually, you know. That's gross. But your eyes? The way you look at me. Love me back. Unconditionally. Your warmth.

*(*KALEF *returns with desert.* JONTHAN *feeds it to her.)*

JONATHAN: The way we can be together without having to talk about it. I mean, since we've been together I've told you more, spoken to you more than I ever have to anybody in my life. I envy you. Next life I'm coming back as a dog. No worries, no cares, just unconditional love and an overwhelming desire to please. I don't know though, trying to please people, make people happy, I don't think that's for me. It's too hard. Maybe next time I'll come back as a fish.

(The scene changes to the dog run.)

*(*JONTHAN *is in the dog run with* KALEF. DANA *enters with* WOOFER *[a dog played by a human] on a leash.* DANA *removes the leash from* WOOFER *who begins to run around excitedly.)*

DANA: O K Woofer, go play. Try not to get any doggy diseases.

*(*WOOFER *spends some time sniffing about as* KALEF *remains aloof.* DANA *scopes out* JONTHAN *though he doesn't notice.* DANA *approaches* JONTHAN *as* WOOFER *approaches* KALEF. DANA *speaks to* JONTHAN *and* WOOFER *speaks to* KALEF. WOOFER *is very horny.*

DANA: Is that your dog?

WOOFER: *(To* KALEF, *saying hi)* Woof.

JONATHAN: Yeah.

DANA: He's so cute.

WOOFER: *(You're cute)* Argh-rough.

JONATHAN: She.

DANA: How old is she?

JONATHAN: What?

WOOFER: *(Are you of legal age)* Grrrgh-rough!

JONATHAN: I don't know.

DANA: *(Suddenly on the verge of tears)* Oh no. Is she a rescue dog?

WOOFER: I'll rescue you.

JONATHAN: I guess.

KALEF: I beg your pardon!?

*(*KALEF *slaps* WOOFER *but it looks like puppies playing at swatting.)*

DANA: Oh look, they like each other. Where did you find her?

JONATHAN: You wouldn't believe me if I told you.

WOOFER: You are unbelievable.

DANA: Oh God, I know. The stories you hear. How can people be so cruel? They tie their animals up....

WOOFER: I'd like to tie you up.

DANA: Leave them for days. I'd like to just take one of those people and rrrggh.

JONATHAN: Right.

KALEF: Yeah, right.

*(*KALEF *walks away from* WOOFER.*)*

DANA: Do you think it's true that owners look like their pets?

WOOFER: You are gorgeous!

JONATHAN: I guess.

DANA: Because I think your dog is very cute.

WOOFER: I have got to fuck you. Come here. Woofer starts chasing Kalef who scampers away playing hard to get.

JONATHAN: Thanks.

DANA: Look. They really like each other. They play so well together.

WOOFER: I wanna give it to you doggy style baby, come here you sweet smellin' bitch.

*(*WOOFER *has caught up to* KALEF *and bends her over and starts humping her from behind.* DANA *runs over and swats* WOOFER *away.)*

DANA: Woofer, bad dog, get off of her.

WOOFER: What? What the? Oh come on. What does a guy have to do to get a little action around here?

KALEF: You know a girl likes a little romance first. A little foreplay.

JONATHAN: I should take her home.

DANA: Oh, do you live around here?

JONATHAN: Yeah.

DANA: Well maybe I'll see you again here at the dog run.

JONATHAN: I doubt it.

WOOFER: Come on, we don't have time for that, let's just do it right here with everyone watching.

*(*JONTHAN *starts putting* KALEF *on her leash.)*

DANA: I'm here every day at this time. You could set your watch by it.

JONATHAN: I'm not nuts about the dog run.

DANA: Really? Why not? It's such a brilliant way to waste time.

JONATHAN: It's like it's own little frigin community but all anybody ever talks about is dogs. Nobody knows each other's names, but they know all the dogs names.

DANA: What's your name?

JONATHAN: ...Jonathan.

DANA: I'm Dana. Nice to meet you. It's hard to connect with people in this city. If a dog gives you something in common...

JONATHAN: Yeah but these people'd watch their neighbor choke to death on a chicken bone but would do anything to save one of these dogs. It's bizarre. How having a dog gives one person permission to talk to another person is completely beyond me.

DANA: Do we need permission to / talk to each other?

JONATHAN: That's why I like poetry.

DANA: You read poetry?

JONATHAN: I write it.

DANA: You do? Wow.

JONATHAN: It lets you communicate. Honestly. Beyond honestly. But you never have to deal with anyone else.

DANA: But don't you communicate when someone reads the poem?

JONATHAN: What if noone ever reads the poem?

DANA: Then it's not a poem, it's just...writing.

JONATHAN: What?

DANA: You look at a Picasso in a museum and it's art. In that moment it's art. But go home and turn off the lights in the museum and it's just a painting hanging on a wall. Art exists in time. That's all it is, is the communication between artist and audience.

JONATHAN: And so an unread poem is just...

DANA: A wasted opportunity.

JONATHAN: Are you an artist?

DANA: No, I sell Porsches.

JONATHAN: Oh.

(Pause)

DANA: Can I ask you something?

JONATHAN: Yeah?

DANA: You seem a little sad.

JONATHAN: I do?

DANA: Yeah.

JONATHAN: I'm not.

DANA: O K. Sorry. Didn't mean to pry.

JONATHAN: Bye.

DANA: Bye.

*(*JONTHAN *and* KALEF *start to exit.* WOOFER *calls after* KALEF *like Marlon Brando.)*

WOOFER: Just give me one more chance. I can change. I'll make you happy, I swear, I'll make you happy. Arrr-Roooo!

*(*DANA *and* WOOFER *watch* JONTHAN *and* KALEF *exit.)*

(Lights)

(The setting changes to SAM's *office.* SAM *and* JONTHAN *are having a session.)*

JONATHAN: Do I seem sad to you?

SAM: Why do you ask?

JONATHAN: I met this girl yesterday. She said I seem sad.

SAM: What do you think made her say that?

JONATHAN: I don't know. She was nice. I actually... talked to her. I thought I was just telling her what I thought but somehow that made her think I was sad.

SAM: What was it you said that might have given her that impression?

JONATHAN: I don't know. I just told her I didn't like the dog run.

SAM: Did it upset you, that she thought you were sad?

JONATHAN: Yeah. I mean, I'm not sad.

SAM: Why does it matter to you if she thinks you're sad, if you think you're not sad?

JONATHAN: I'm not sad.

SAM: So then?

JONATHAN: I don't know. I guess I just wanted her to think better of me than that.

SAM: Is she someone you could see again?

JONATHAN: I guess.

SAM: Maybe you could try to clear things up.

JONATHAN: Is it worth the effort?

SAM: Is it worth the effort? You know I had a client in here the other day. Little younger than you. I'm not betraying anything by telling you this. He read me a poem his Father had written for him when he was one year old. And I thought, "That's amazing". A Father makes the effort to write a poem and his son keeps it with him twenty years later. Can you imagine the bond those two men must have? So yes Jonathan, I think it's worth the effort.

(The setting changes to JONTHAN*'s apartment.* JONTHAN *and* KALEF *watch T V and eat Chinese food.)*

JONATHAN: Pass me a dumpling.

*(*KALEF *does. They eat together playfully, flirtatiously, perhaps feeding each other.* JONTHAN *doesn't really hear* KALEF *talk, it's more like he is speaking a monologue while intuiting her reactions.)*

JONATHAN: Why are people such a pain in the ass?

*(*KALEF *shrugs her shoulders.)*

JONATHAN: Sometimes I think you actually do know.
Why do people want to talk about everything?
You never want to talk about anything.

KALEF: Why do you want to be left alone?

JONATHAN: I don't know. I just think other people are stupid.

KALEF: No.

JONATHAN: No. I guess I feel like I'll screw it up. Do it wrong. "It's better to be thought a fool and keep your mouth shut, than open it and remove all doubt."

KALEF: "It is better to have loved and lost than never loved at all".

JONATHAN: Sometimes I just wish I could be invisible you know? Do you? Kalef? Kalef kalef kalef.
(He addresses the audience.)
My hands.
MY FUCKING HANDS!
I mean
I could feel them,
feel what I touched,

Feel the feel
of my face
with the end of my arm,
But I
could not
see them.

(He looks at KALEF *who is looking away seeming oblivious.)*

JONATHAN: I went to a mirror
To see for myself
and there was my shirt,
everything normal,
but no head.
No me.
NO FUCKING ME!
I was simply gone.
Clothes moving
on a missing mannequin.
I couldn't believe
believe it.
It was the weirdest feeling in the world.
I dropped my clothes
and stood there
naked.
Really
naked.
A nakedness no man has known.
I wanted to observe
everything,
knowing noone could
observe
me back.
I could
partake
of society
without
having to

participate.
I could
do things
I could never
do
before,
because,
in fact,
there was
no I.
I was a ghost.
I had to be careful
I had to find a way of acting
without
inter
acting.

(The scene starts to change.)

JONATHAN: I suddenly became very afraid that the military would start looking for me. There was only one place I could think to go where I would be completely unnoticed. The dog run.

*(*JONTHAN *enters the dog run where* DANA *is standing next to* WOOFER *with a plastic bag over her hand.* WOOFER *is crouching.)*

WOOFER: Urgh.

DANA: Come on Woofer, you can do it.

WOOFER: Argh.

DANA: Poop for Mommy, there you go.

WOOFER: Oooh.

DANA: Good boy. Good boy.

(He poops. Comically. She picks up the poop in a bag and throws it away. WOOFER *walks around a bit then becomes suspicious. Smells something. He walks right up to*

JONTHAN *[who* DANA *of course does not notice] and looks him right in the eye.)*

WOOFER: Woof.

*(*JONTHAN *backs away.)*

WOOFER: I said: Woof.

DANA: Woofer? What is up with you? Calm down, freak toast. There's nothing there, what are you barking at?

WOOFER: Woof. Woof. Woof.

*(*JONTHAN *reaches his hand out.* WOOFER *smells it.* JONTHAN *pets* WOOFER.*)*

DANA: Come on, time for some food.

*(*DANA *puts* WOOFER *on a leash and they exit.)*

JONATHAN: I followed her.
I
couldn't help it.
I
could do it
So
I did do it.
I followed her home,
when she opened her door,
I stole
my way into her apartment.
It wasn't for sex,
I didn't want to see her
naked
in the shower or anything,
and it wasn't to scare her,
I didn't want to hear her
Scream
Or anything.
I never wanted her

to know
That I was there.
It was just...
to be with her
without having to...
actually...
be with her.

*(*DANA *sits in her apartment drinking wine.* WOOFER *sleeps off somewhere on the floor.* JONTHAN *watches her.)*

JONATHAN: There was something about her alright.
So comfortable
alone
inside her body.
At peace inside her solitude.
Alone,
but never lonely.

*(*DANA *puts on some slow music and slowly begins to dance to it. She is not a great dancer and she is not trying to impress anyone, but she is lost in the song, completely unaware of her surroundings and surrendering to the flow of the music. Jonathan watches, impressed. He gets up and dances with her though of course she is oblivious. He is able to mimic her moves and have his body compliment hers, but he never touches her. They end up dancing beautifully together.)*

JONATHAN: I wanted
to touch her.
I wanted
to speak.
I hope you understand,
This was a
frighteningly foreign feeling.
I knew
that if
I did,

I'd break the spell.
Because
The thing that
truly
allured me to her
was that she couldn't
see me.

(The music stops. DANA *exits.)*

JONATHAN: When she went to sleep
I left.
In the morning she'd
chastise
herself for not remembering to lock the door. She'd
recall the previous night with fondness. That fantastic,
just right, feeling of being completely alone
yet
completely connected.
I had to
see her
again.
The problem of course
was simply that she
couldn't
see me.
My condition
did not
appear
to be reversible.
And then I had an idea. I went on-line and ordered
new dog tags for Kalef; ones with my phone number
on them. "Dogtags-at-your-doorstepdot-com" or
something brought them within the hour.
God bless America.

(The scene begins to change to the dog run.)

JONATHAN: I took Kalef to the dog run and I waited.

*(*DANA *and* WOOFER *enter.* DANA *lets* WOOFER *off the leash.* WOOFER *runs right up to* KALEF *and sniffs her.)*

WOOFER: Hey, baby, long time no see. But I knew you couldn't resist me.

*(*DANA *walks up to* KALEF.*)*

DANA: Hey, you're Jonathan's dog.

JONATHAN: She remembered my name.

DANA: How did you get lost in here?

WOOFER: Get lost with me, I'll make all your dreams come true.

JONATHAN: She waited awhile to see if I'd show.

DANA: Well, I guess you're coming with me.

*(*DANA *takes the strap off her purse, turns it into a leash, puts* KALEF *on it, and leads the two dogs away.* KALEF *looks sadly back at* JONTHAN.*)*

KALEF: You're not leaving me are you?

JONATHAN: I'll see you soon.

(The scene begins to change. DANA *and the dogs are gone.)*

JONATHAN: I ran home and waited by the phone.

*(*JONTHAN *on one side of the stage with a phone,* DANA *on the other side with a phone.)*

DANA: Hi, is this Jonathan?

JONATHAN: Yes.

DANA: I don't know if you remember me. This is Dana from the dog run?

JONATHAN: Dana.

DANA: I sell Porsche's and say inappropriate, pretentious things about art?

JONATHAN: I remember.

DANA: Um, well I found your dog.

JONATHAN: You did? Oh my God that's great. Where?

DANA: In the dog run actually. Did you leave her there?

JONATHAN: No. No, of course not. She somehow got out of my apartment. She's like a Houdini dog. She must have gone there cause that's her favorite place.

DANA: Weird. Well. Anyway. She's O K.

JONATHAN: Oh that's great. Can I come pick her up?

DANA: Sure.

JONATHAN: I'll be over in a few minutes.

DANA: Wait. Let me give you my address.

JONATHAN: Oh. Right. Of course.

(DANA exits. JONTHAN begins dressing as he describes.)

JONATHAN: *(To the audience)*
Life imitates art.
I did the only thing I knew to do.
Long trench coat.
Hat. Scarf. Gloves.
Big sunglasses.
You couldn't tell I was invisible.
You could only tell I was a freak.

(JONTHAN steps into DANA's apartment. DANA does notice that he looks like a bit of a freak.)

JONATHAN: Oh God there she is.

(KALEF gives JONTHAN a big hug and starts kissing him.)

JONATHAN: Hi. I know, I missed you too. I didn't know where you were. I was so worried about you. *(To DANA)* Thank you so much.

DANA: Sure. No problem.

JONATHAN: *(To KALEF)* Sit. Stay.

*(*KALEF *sits on the floor and watches the scene from there.)*

JONATHAN: Where's Woofer?

DANA: Sleeping. When he's sleeping it's best not to wake him.

JONATHAN: *(Reaching for his wallet)* I feel like I should give you a reward or something.

DANA: No. Don't be a dork. That's retarted.

JONATHAN: I'm just so... Thanks a lot. Can I at least take you to dinner or something?

DANA: Sure. Yeah. That'd be nice.

JONATHAN: O K. Great.

DANA: Are you O K?

JONATHAN: Yeah.

DANA: I mean, why are you dressed like that?

JONATHAN: You can never be too careful right?

DANA: Right.

JONATHAN: Right.

DANA: Careful about...what exactly?

JONATHAN: I don't think you'd believe me if I told you.

DANA: Try me.

JONATHAN: Maybe I should show you. But prepare yourself.

DANA: O K.

JONATHAN: Don't freak out O K?

DANA: O K.

JONATHAN: It's weird, but I mean, it's just...

DANA: It's O K, just show me.

*(*JONTHAN *takes off the hat, sunglasses and scarf.)*

DANA: Oh my God.

JONATHAN: I know.

DANA: How do you do that?

JONATHAN: I don't know.

DANA: That is supremely weird.

JONATHAN: I know.

DANA: You don't... know how you're doing that?

JONATHAN: No.

DANA: Come on.

(DANA goes over and touches his invisible head. She screams really loudly.)

JONATHAN: Shhh.

DANA: Sorry. That's just...I just had to get that out. You weren't like that the other day.

JONATHAN: It's a relatively new development.

DANA: Well make it stop.

JONATHAN: I can't.

DANA: Is the rest of you like this too?

JONATHAN: Yes.

DANA: Have you seen a doctor?

JONATHAN: No.

DANA: Well... I don't know what to say. You've turned into the invisible man.

JONATHAN: That about sums it up.

DANA: That is supremely weird Jonathan. Can you please put your glasses back on or something so I can at least look at or...near your eyes.

(He does.)

DANA: Thanks. You need to...show this to someone.

JONATHAN: Does this change our dinner plan?

DANA: Well it might be a bit awkward to go out with someone who's invisible.

JONATHAN: We could have dinner at my place.

DANA: That's not exactly the point. You're going to need to deal with this.

JONATHAN: I was sort of hoping to stay like this.

DANA: Invisible?

JONATHAN: Yes.

DANA: Jonathan you can't be invisible.

JONATHAN: But I am invisible.

DANA: I mean, O K, you can be invisible, or you at least can be invisible, but you can't...I don't know... participate as an invisible. Especially if you don't want to tell anyone.

JONATHAN: What does telling anyone have to do with it?

DANA: Well...at least if you told someone you would be participating because being invisible is pretty...different and I think people would be interested to talk to you about it.

JONATHAN: I don't want to talk to anyone about it.

DANA: Exactly.

JONATHAN: I want to stay like this.

DANA: Why?

JONATHAN: I thought if I were invisible it might make things easier.

DANA: How?

JONATHAN: I'm not sure. I thought we could be together better if I was invisible.

DANA: That makes no sense to me.

JONATHAN: I know. I'm sorry. I don't really know how to be with people. I want to, but...well, like with my Mother, maybe I could just be with her without her talking at me all the time. I'd like to see what she's like when she's quiet.

DANA: But maybe that's not what she wants. Maybe she likes to talk.

JONATHAN: Well, I don't know, I thought you might like being invisible too.

DANA: I don't think so.

JONATHAN: You might. I've seen you, when you're alone. When you're alone you're different, at peace. Like being invisible.

DANA: You've seen me when I'm alone?! What are you some sort of sick pervert?!

JONATHAN: No, I just...

DANA: Spying on me?! Were you!? Get out. Get the fuck out of my apartment. Y, you're an invisible freak.

(He quickly throws down his sunglasses, removes his jacket and steps out of his shoes. He is now totally invisible to her.)

DANA: What are you doing? Hey. That's not funny. Where are you? This is really creeping me out.

(She flails and swings her arms as if to try to hit him, he dodges away from her.)

DANA: Stop it. This is creepy. Woofer, Woofer.

*(*WOOFER *runs in.)*

DANA: Sick 'em boy.

*(*WOOFER *growls right at* JONTHAN. KALEF *gets up and readies herself to protect* JONTHAN.*)*

DANA: Get out of my apartment. You're sick. You need help. Leave me alone you fucking weirdo. Woofer is he gone?

(Lights change. DANA *and* WOOFER *exit.* JONTHAN *addresses the audience.)*

JONATHAN: It wasn't the reception I'd expected.
I held Kalef by the scruff of her neck
and started walking home
pondering my fate.
And then I saw a car heading straight for me.
I thought,
"surely he'll stop,
I'm standing right in front of him
Surely he'll see..."
then I remembered my condition
and I screamed:
"SEE ME!,
PLEASE SEE ME!"

(The sound of the same pile up)

EPILOGUE:
THE POLICE INTERROGATION ROOM

*(*MARLENE *sits with her head in her hands.* ABE, CATHY, *and* JONTHAN *are, for the first time, not present.* DON *enters.)*

DON: Hey.

*(*MARLENE *looks up.)*

DON: You O K?

MARLENE: What? Yeah, just tired. What's up?

DON: I just got a call from the coroner's office. None of them made it.

MARLENE: The car accident?

DON: Yeah.

MARLENE: The old guy, the woman, and the naked guy?

DON: None of them.

MARLENE: Anymore eyewitnesses?

DON: Just our loopy one.

MARLENE: And...?

(DON *consults the file.)*

DON: His final statement: He claims that the old guy driving the car was about eighteen, and that this woman was like a model or something, and that the naked guy just materialized out of thin air. Not the most reliable. Wish we had more.

MARLENE: No point in wishing.

DON: Yeah.

MARLENE: Hey, what about the dog?

DON: Who the hell knows at this point?

MARLENE: And why do you think that guy was naked?

DON: Guess we'll never know now.

MARLENE: It doesn't really matter I suppose. People are crazy. And then they die. *(She rubs her head.)*

DON: Hey, you O K?

MARLENE: Yeah, you know, just life, whatever.

DON: Yeah. Doesn't get any easier does it?

MARLENE: Nope.

DON: Where's Superman to come rescue us?

MARLENE: Fly us away and out of our misery?

DON: Sounds good.

MARLENE: I don't think he's coming.

DON: Nope.

MARLENE: I want Superpowers.

DON: Sure.

MARLENE: But now they're...

DON: What?

MARLENE: Whatever.

DON: You want to get a cup of coffee and talk about it?

MARLENE: Superpowers?

DON: No.

MARLENE: I don't want to...

DON: What?

MARLENE: I don't know. Burden you.

DON: Marlene?

MARLENE: What?

DON: Look at me.

(She does.)

DON: You want to talk about it?

MARLENE: Alright. Sure. Thanks. Yeah, I do.

(She gets up. They start to go. There is a scratching at the door.)

DON: The fuck is that?

MARLENE: Who cares?

DON: Should we get it?

MARLENE: Get it? No. Let someone else get it. I need a cup of coffee.

*(*MARLENE *and* DON *exit. The scratching continues. As the lights fade to black.)*

END OF PLAY

www.ingramcontent.com/pod-product-compliance
Lightning Source LLC
Chambersburg PA
CBHW070025110426
42741CB00034B/2532

* 9 7 8 0 8 8 1 4 5 2 6 4 8 *